Animal Naps

Cataloging Information

Ham, Catherine.
    Animal naps/Catherine Ham
        32 p. : col. ill. ; 20 cm.
    Includes index (p.).
    Summary: Uses verse and photographs to explore sleep and sleep-
        related behavior in animals. Includes a range of taxa,
        including mammals, amphibians, birds, reptiles, and
        fish.
    LC: QL755.3 .C65
    Dewey: 591.56 22
    ISBN-13: 978-0-9832014-1-0 (alk. paper)
        Sleep —Juvenile literature

Cover Design: Stewart Pack
Art Director: Celia Naranjo
Copy Editor: Tina Miller
Photo Research: Dawn Cusick

10 9 8 7 6 5 4 3 2 1

First edition

Published by EarlyLight Books, Inc.
1436 Dellwood Road
Waynesville, NC 28786

To Jane . . .

ISBN-13: 978-0-9832014-1-0

Animal Naps

Catherine
Ham

 EarlyLight Books

WAYNESVILLE, NORTH CAROLINA, USA

Animal Naps

All kinds of creatures
Are taking their naps
Leopards and lizards
Big bears and bats
Snoozing, sleeping
Eyes shut, no peeping
Hedgehogs and hippos...
Their bedtimes need keeping

Sssssshh!

Cute puppies so soundly napping
Ssssh! Quietly... Don't make a din
Do you think that maybe they're dreaming
Of growing to fit into their skin?

Mother fox prepares a den
When she has cubs she cares for
But a fox on his own
Won't make a special home
Almost any place will do
For a fox to doze alone

He goes searching for a spot
That he really likes a lot
Wraps his warm tail round his face
Settling in his sleeping space

TAIL PILLOW!

Is the light bothering this 'roo
Do you think?
As he lies taking his nap
Is he trying to cover his eyes
Do you think?
Perhaps he should wear a cap?

If you'd been out walking
And seen this chap...
Oh my goodness, WHAT a surprise!

SWEET
DREAMS

The leopard's a creature of speed
Who can run like the wind if there's need
When she'd like a little rest
A high branch is just the best
You could say that this leopard's been treed!

CAT NAP

A bear will sleep deep in his Winter den
But when the weather's warmer
Then
This rather large chap
Will take his nap
In any cool place he can find

To keep out of the heat
When he's eaten his meat
He does quite like to snooze
What spot will he choose...?
He really doesn't mind

SNORE

A polar bear
Will nap anywhere
But always in snow or on ice
In the cold freezing North
She spends her whole life
For her I suppose
That must be very nice
But it's not somewhere
That I want to go!

Sssssssssssssh!
Tread lightly on your tippy-toes
Please don't make a sound
Let the mama and her baby doze
Gently on the ground

MAMA HUGS

SOUTH AMERICAN SLEEPER!

What is this creature
You see sleeping here?
It isn't a pig
And it's sure not a deer

It can run very fast
And it swims very well
Though its eyesight is poor
It's got a great sense of smell

These animals are big
But endangered, I fear
We're doing all that we can
To protect the TAPIR

SIESTA!

Here's some hippo info
Which might be new to you
In ancient Greek the hippo's name
Means the same as "river horse"

Of course, we know this isn't so
It's true it's not a horse
But the massive hippo lumbers
With a most impressive force

Did you know a hippo slumbers
With its nostrils underwater?
While still asleep, it doesn't wake
It rises up, a breath to take ....

It just seems to know it oughta!

SLUMBER!

A koala often sleeps
In the fork of a tree
Which seems sort of strange
To you and to me

She's a rather picky eater
Eats eucalyptus leaves
There is no way she can change
And eat like you and me

She will rest and nap and snooze
Many hours in every day
But she'll never choose to sleep
In any other way

SLEEP TIGHT!

TREE SLEEPER

A sloth's not much good on the ground
He spends his whole life in a tree
He keeps hanging around
Likes to sleep upside-down
Should we give that a try, you and me?

An adorable monkey, completely whacked out
She must feel quite safe to be so sacked out
Way up high in her tree you would think she might fall
Not at all

She's totally adapted to life in the trees
Her fur gently ruffled by a whispering breeze
Way up high in her tree
With the leaves for a sheet
And her blanket the sky

LIFE IS Goooooooooood . . .

This Red Panda needs a rest
So that his tummy can digest
The food he loves the best:
Bamboo

A little bigger than a cat
He likes a forest habitat
There's a couple of odd things
That he will do

He uses his front paws
To put his food between his jaws
Could be berries, could be eggs,
A bird or two

I bet you cannot think
How he gets water for a drink?
From a puddle, from a pond, from a stream.
He will sit down next to it
Dip his paws in it a bit
Then lick the water off until they're clean

BALANCING
ACT . . .

17

DOZY

Have you ever thought
How a hedgehog got her name?
Well, her little face is like a pig's
They're very much the same
A pig is sometimes called a hog
And a hedgehog often digs
Under a hedge or hollow log
Or wiggles under some twigs
There in her cozy nest
She'll snooze for most of the day
Taking her dozy rest
Sleeping snugly and safely away

WARMLY WRAPPED!

A bat is not a mouse
Nor it he a bird
He's just the oddest animal
Of which you've ever heard

He takes flight at early night
On his very special wings
Which can fold like an umbrella
They're the most amazing things

A bat sleeps upside down
In large groups or quite alone
With his feet he clings on tight...
But please, don't try this at home!

HIDE & SLEEP

This lovely little treefrog
Hidden by a leaf
Has no idea we see her
Sleeping underneath

She's all sorts of stunning colors
Green, blue, orange, yellow, white
It seems her bulging red eyes
Give her perfect dark-night sight

All day while she's napping
Nothing much will come a-zapping
But if she's woken in the day ...
They'll POP her enemy a fright!

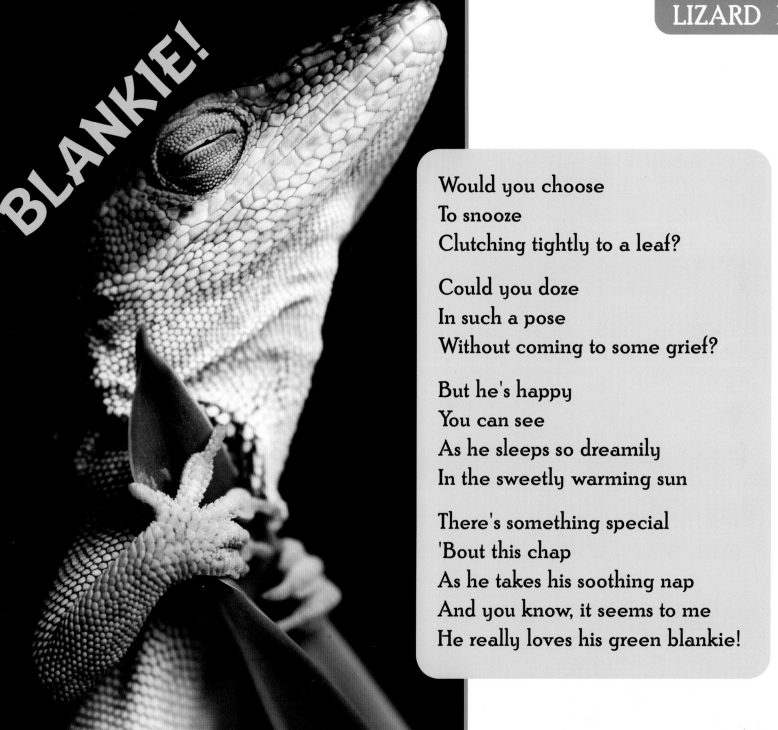

BLANKIE!

Would you choose
To snooze
Clutching tightly to a leaf?

Could you doze
In such a pose
Without coming to some grief?

But he's happy
You can see
As he sleeps so dreamily
In the sweetly warming sun

There's something special
'Bout this chap
As he takes his soothing nap
And you know, it seems to me
He really loves his green blankie!

RELAX!

This beautiful bird's a flamingo
And she's standing there sleeping, by jingo
She's napping just fine
On one leg at a time
With her head tucked up under her wing~o

Most ducks doze on water
It keeps the predators away
Half the duck's brain stays awake
Is what the scientists say

You have a bed
And a pillow for your head
But with their feathers fluffed up
Warm air puffed up
Standing on one leg
Heads tucked under tight
Ducks sleep on the frozen water
Safely through the night

SNUGLY WARM

DREAMING?

There are many different types of seals
In oceans, lakes and seas
Most time they spend in water
Where they sleep with the greatest of ease

When they want to have their babies
They will need to come on shore
But they also love to lie on land
Where they'll nap and gently snore

SLUMBERING ...

A deeply sleeping turtle
Resting on the sand
Turtles mostly live in water
But spend some time on land

Their bodies are protected
By a special bony shell
And some have horny scales
That keep them safe as well

Because a turtle is a reptile
And can't make his body heat
He needs the sun to warm him
Don't you think that's neat?

SUNNY SNOOZE

A boa grows quite amazingly long
Her body is also incredibly strong
She eats lots of rats
And a great many bats
She'll dine on anything happening along

She's sleeping, keeping warm in the day's sunlight
For she's been out hunting,
Creeping through the night
Our boa lives alone
She has no home of her own
But you see she is happy, sleekly curled up tight

An alligator's not the same
As a crocodile
Though they both
Love to doze
For a long, long while

Be it day or be it night
Their sleep's always very light
It's a dreamy sort of lifestyle

BEAUTY SLEEP

DEEP SLEEP

This fish is not a parrot
And a parrot's not a fish
But apart from his name
This fish is really strange
He can rearrange his colors
Just whenever he might wish

His teeth are tightly fused
Into a sort of beak
Used to scratch and tweak
A batch of algae off the rocks.
Yes, I hear you
UGH! Nasty stuff
But it is his favorite dish

He's sleeping soundly now
Seems he can't eat any more
Do you think that he might snore?

Hide and seek!
See us sleep
Tucked among the coral deep

DRIFTING OFF!

ELEPHANT

PRAIRIE DOG

TURTLE DOVE

ORANGUTAN

PIG

POLECAT

CAPYBARA

LION

RACCOON

MONKEY

OTTERS

INDEX

Acknowledgments

Photography by: Anat-Oli, Henk Bentlage, Dean Bertoncelj, Steve Bower, Zbynek Burival, Sascha Burkard, Hung Chung Chih, Kuricheva Ekaterina, Jarrod Erbe, Susan Flashman, Edith Frincu, Eric Isselée, Cathy Keifer, J. Klingebiel, K.L. Kohn, Bartlomiej K. Kwieciszewski, Denise Lafferty, Keith Levit, Richard A. McGuirk, Krzysztof Odziomek, Tomas Pavelka, Terry Poche, Leigh Prather, Serg Salivon, P. Schwarz, Asther Lau Choon Siew, Nikola Spasenoski, Jose Alberto Tejo, David Thyberg, Ostanina Ekaterina Vadimovna, Gert Johannes Jacobus Very, and Heather Wenzel.

Gratitude is also extended to Carole Dennis for sharing sample pages with her sons, Andrew and Michael.